Shapes

and

patterns

PLAY BAC
PUBLISHING

More.Brain.Power

Open your eyes and pay close
attention. You are about to enter
a world of extaordinary
discoveries!

Every shape and every pattern can be found in nature!
Page by page, picture by picture, try and find the look-a-likes. Guess what the
Yorkshire terrier and the shark have in common. Compare the tiger's stripes to
the wild boar and admire the similarities between the pangolin and pinecone.
Then, let yourself be surprised by an amazing chameleon and a homely hippo-
potamus who could use a bath.

You'll find out that nature can be absolutely amazing!

Round

nest

Come take a walk through nature...

owl

cherry

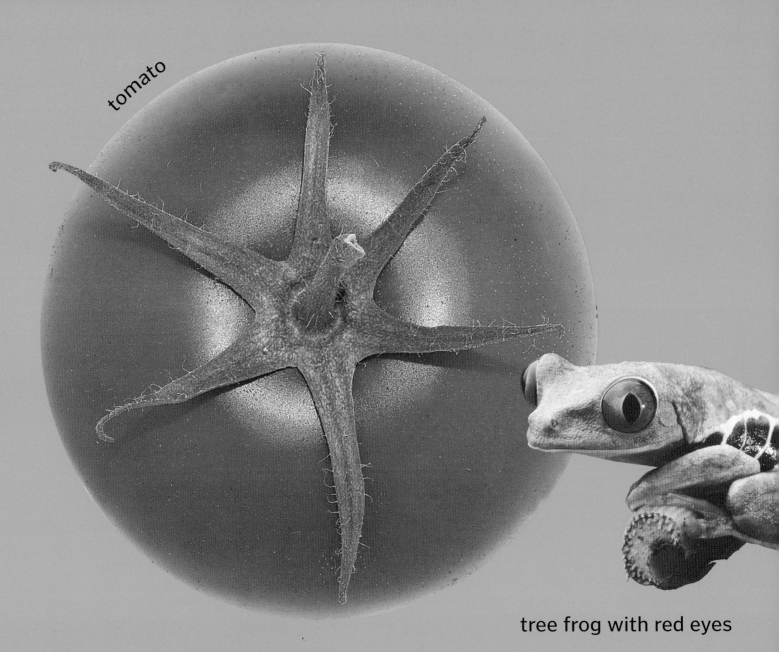

tomato

peas

tree frog with red eyes

... And discover what makes the world go round.

Curved

banana

swan

the moon

orange sections

These graceful curves
are everywhere.

a cat's tail

11

Oval

How about a game of football?

watermelon

grapes

turtle

egg

beetles

"No!" cried the egg.
"I don't want to play ball!"

Cylindrical

baobab trees

corn on the cob

penguin

"Why do you walk on four legs?" asked the penguin of the armadillo. "When it's just as easy to walk on two!"

armadillo

centipede

sugar cane

Lines

asparagus

heron

I'd rather eat an asparagus spear than look like one!

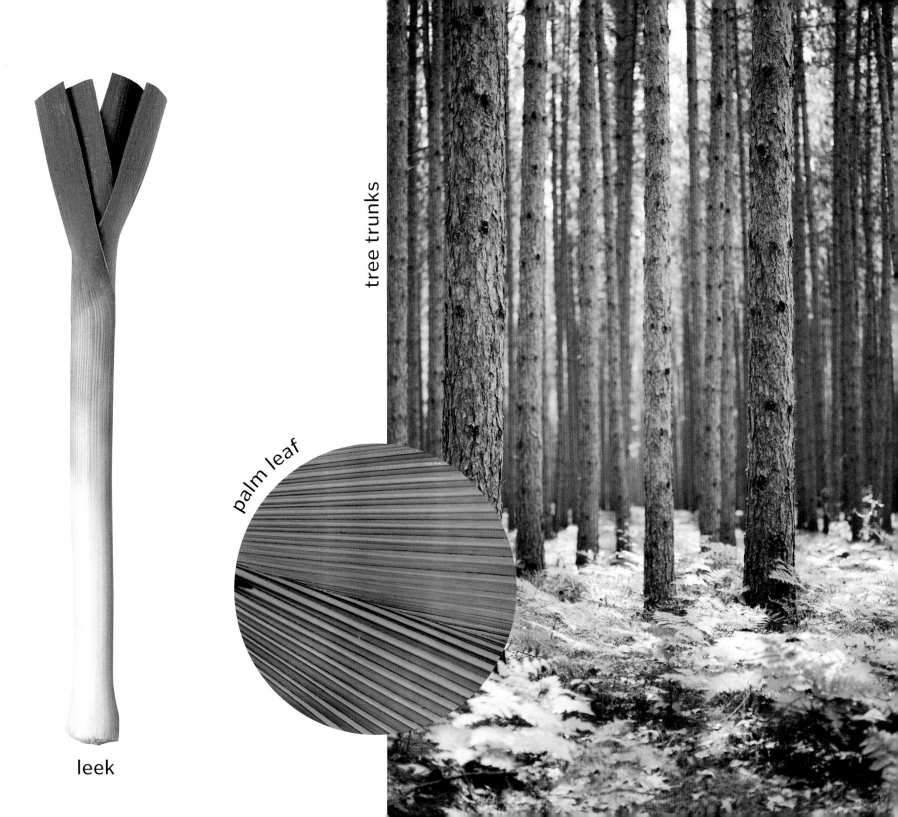

leek

palm leaf

tree trunks

pyrite

Square,

iceberg

Diamond

One, two, three, four
A square has four sides,
Just the same.

One, two, three, four
A diamond's a square,
Standing on its head!

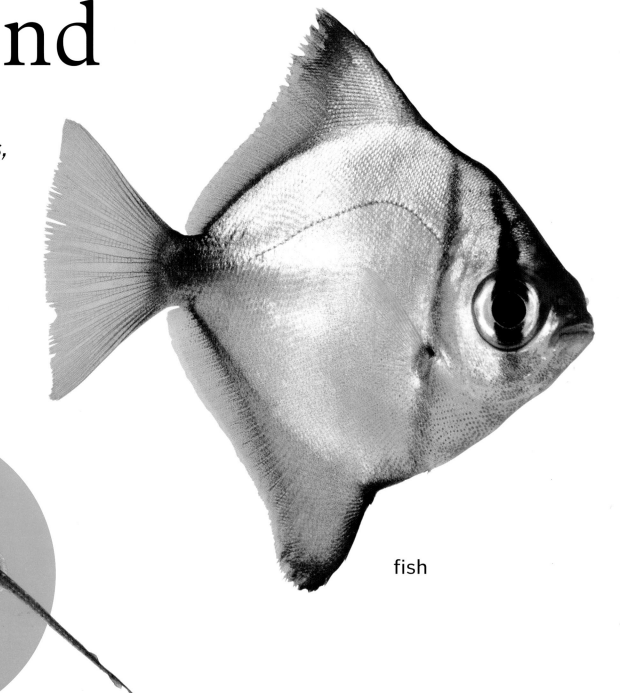

fish

ray

turtle

pineapple

cracked earth

Patterns

Random and repeat patterns show up in the strangest places.

baby giraffe

honeycomb

Yorkshire terrier ear

mountain peak

An unusual shape to have in common, the triangle is number one!

Triangle

shark fin

seashells

Jagged

rooster

leaf

Venus fly trap

Cockadoodle doo
Cockadoodle doo
No, I'm not afraid of you!

iguana

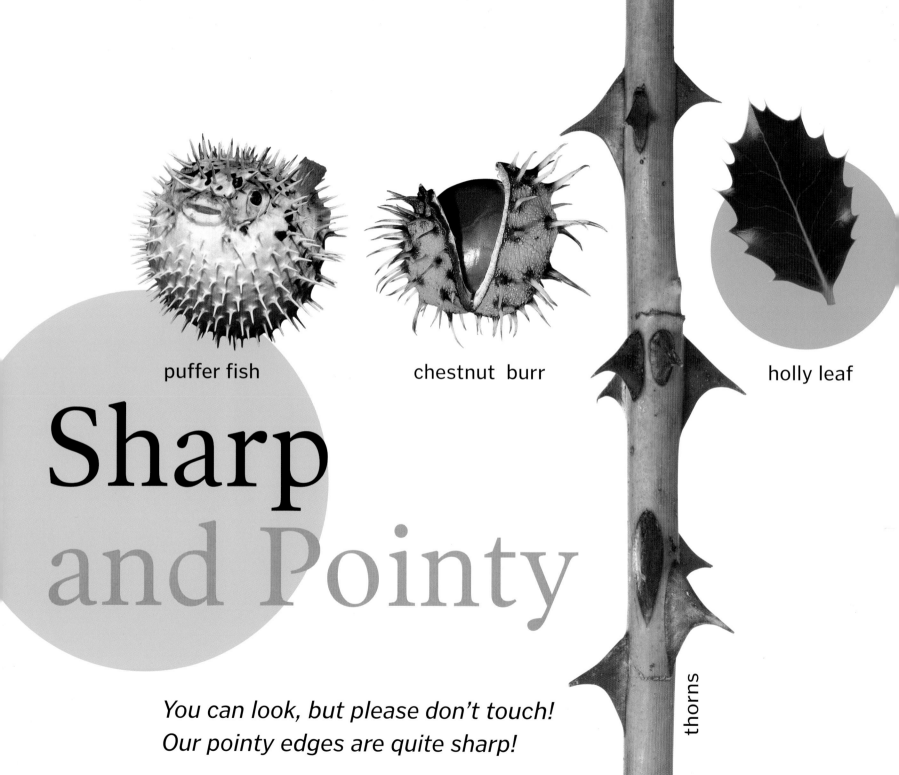

puffer fish

chestnut burr

holly leaf

thorns

Sharp
and Pointy

You can look, but please don't touch!
Our pointy edges are quite sharp!

thistle

woodpecker's beak

hedgehog

Wrinkled
and Wavy

Did somebody hide the iron?

dried chili pepper

shar-pei puppies

walnut

tree bark

morel mushroom

sand

Our wrinkles make us toss and turn.

Hairy

Highland cow

pussy willows

"Be a pal," exclaimed the cow.
"And give me back my comb!"

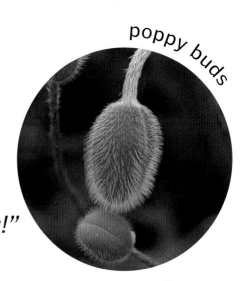
poppy buds

"In a minute," answered the tarantula. *"I'm on my last leg!"*

tarantula

Fine Lines

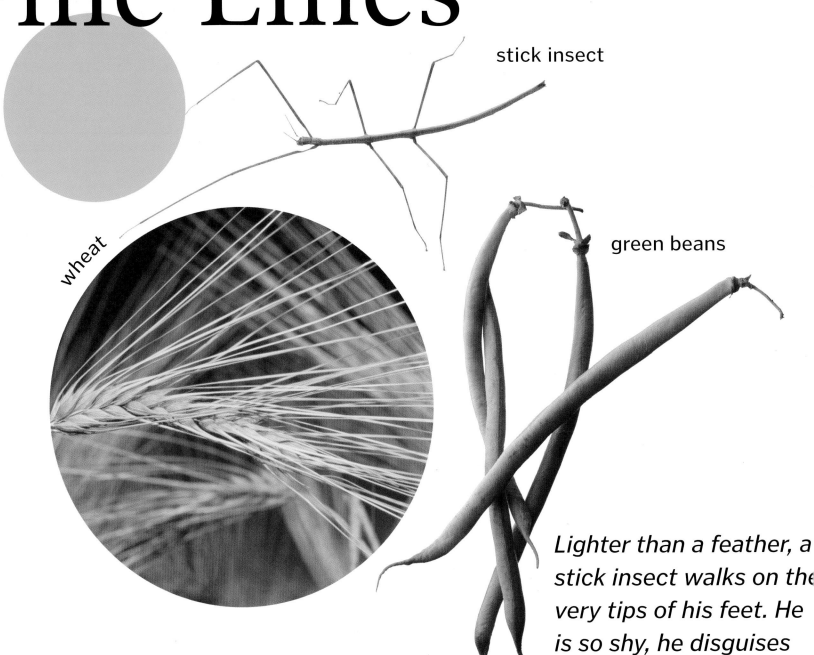

stick insect

wheat

green beans

Lighter than a feather, a stick insect walks on the very tips of his feet. He is so shy, he disguises himself as a twig.

spider web

cabbage leaf

dragonfly

swan feather

Flat and Wide

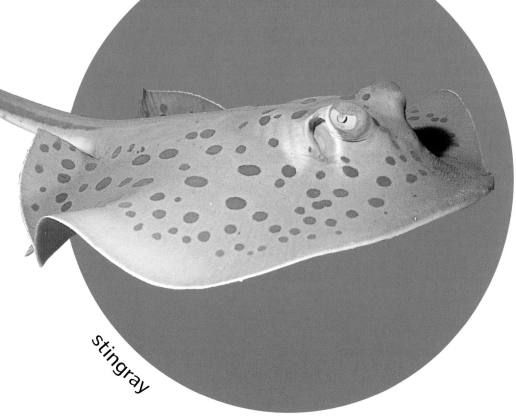

stingray

water lily pads

*Can you please look where you are walking,
Mr. Elephant? You've squished me flat!*

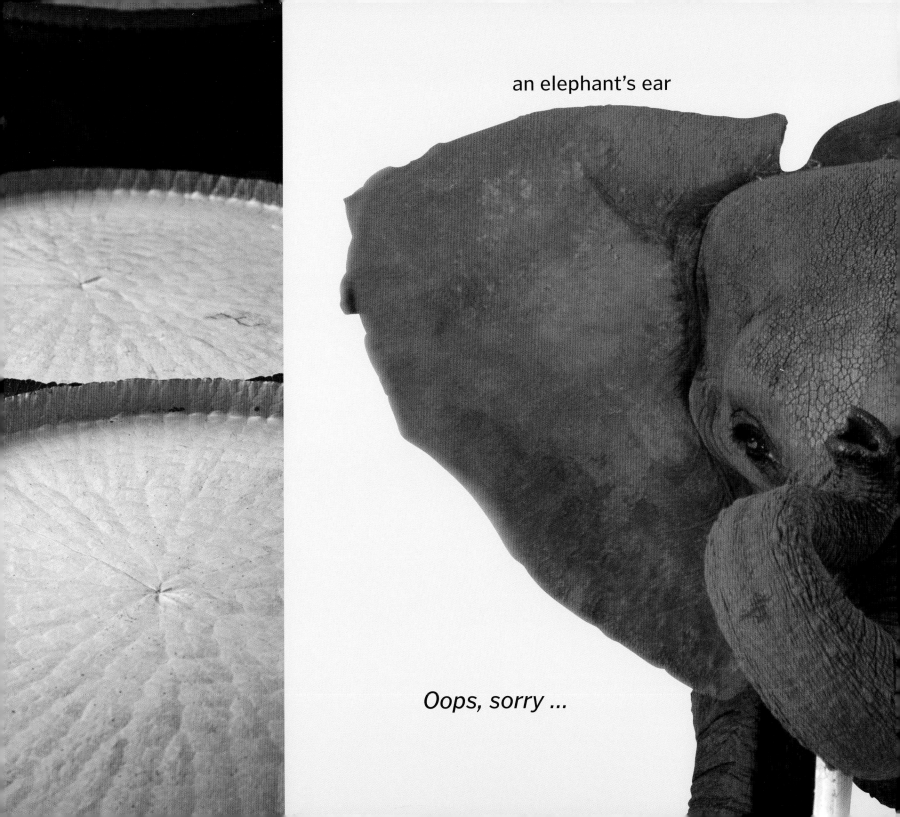

an elephant's ear

Oops, sorry ...

Spatulas

With our flat beaks, we are the best pancake flippers you have ever seen!

spoonbill

platypus

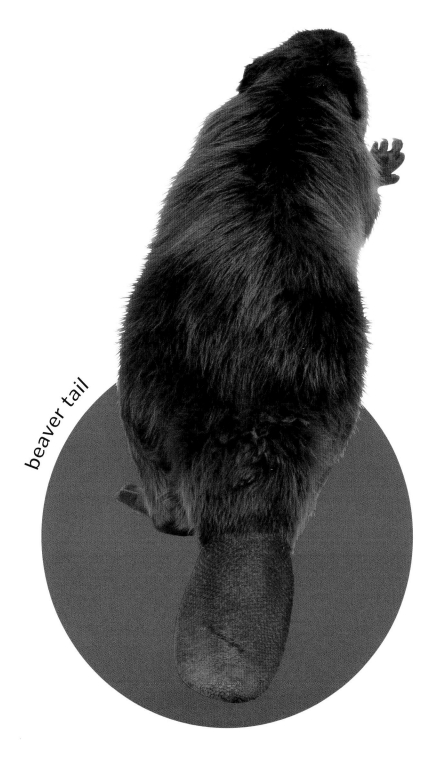

beaver tail

My tail is perfect for spreading butter and jam.

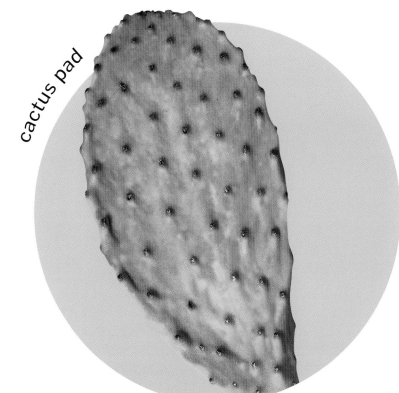

cactus pad

37

starfish

Stars

*Everybody stretch your legs,
your petals and your arms.
Isn't it great to be a star!*

snowflake

star fruit

mushrooms

spider

daffodil

sunflower

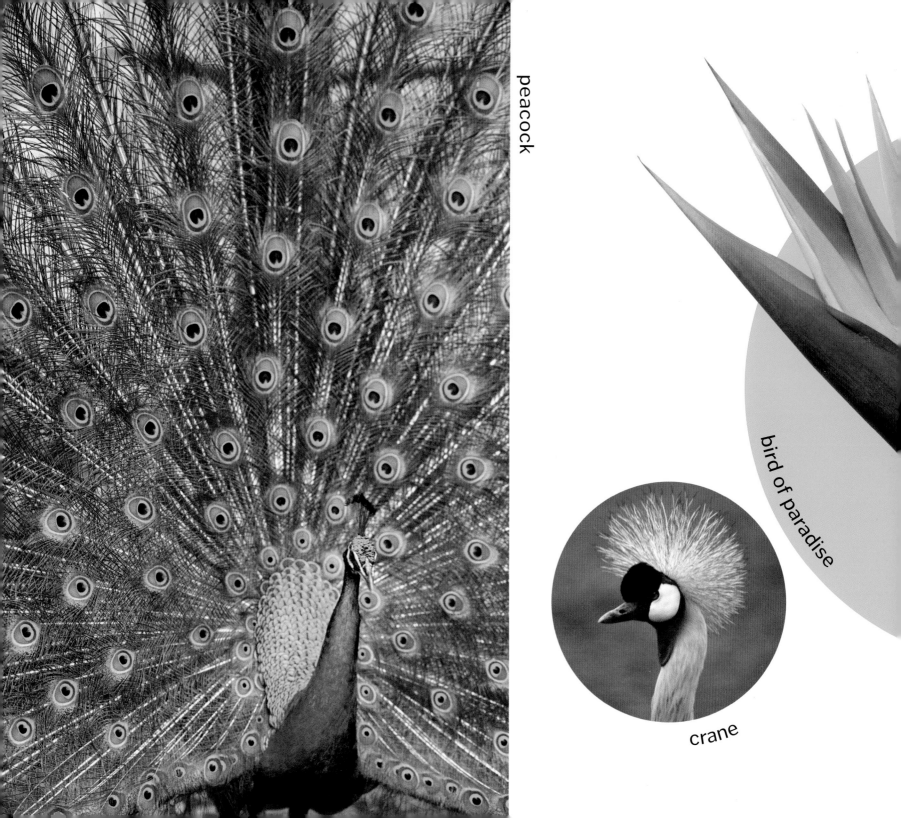

peacock

bird of paradise

crane

Fan-shaped

hummingbird

*Hurry up and get ready ladies,
the ball is about to begin.
And don't forget your fans!*

scallop shell

turkey

Spirals

fiddlehead fern

chameleon

"I'm lost," says the snail. "Can you help me find the garden?"
"It's this way," answers the ram. "Follow my horns."

ram's horn

snail

Scales

Our scales will make you think twice, but underneath we are really quite nice.

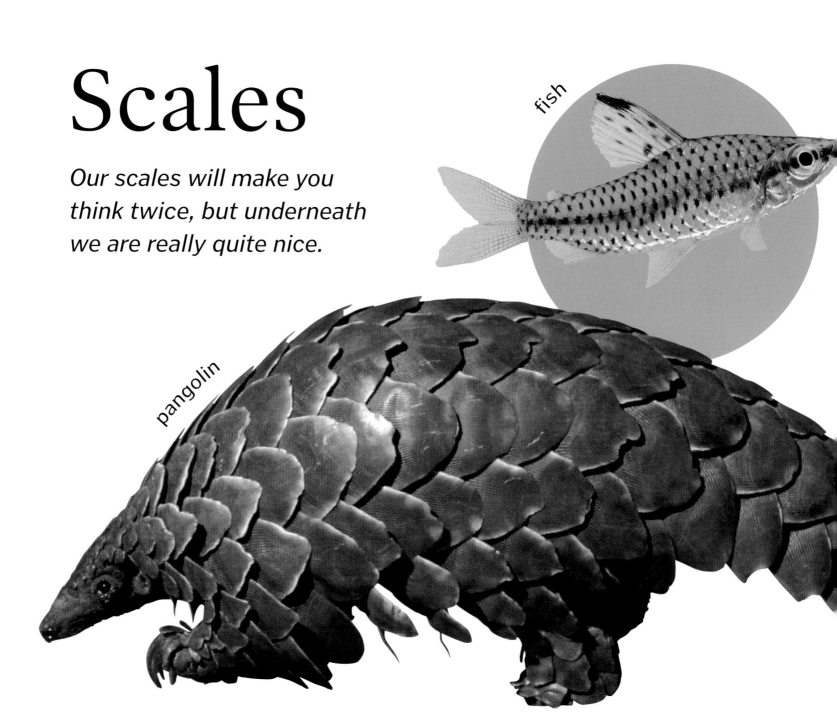

fish

pangolin

mushroom

artichoke

pinecone

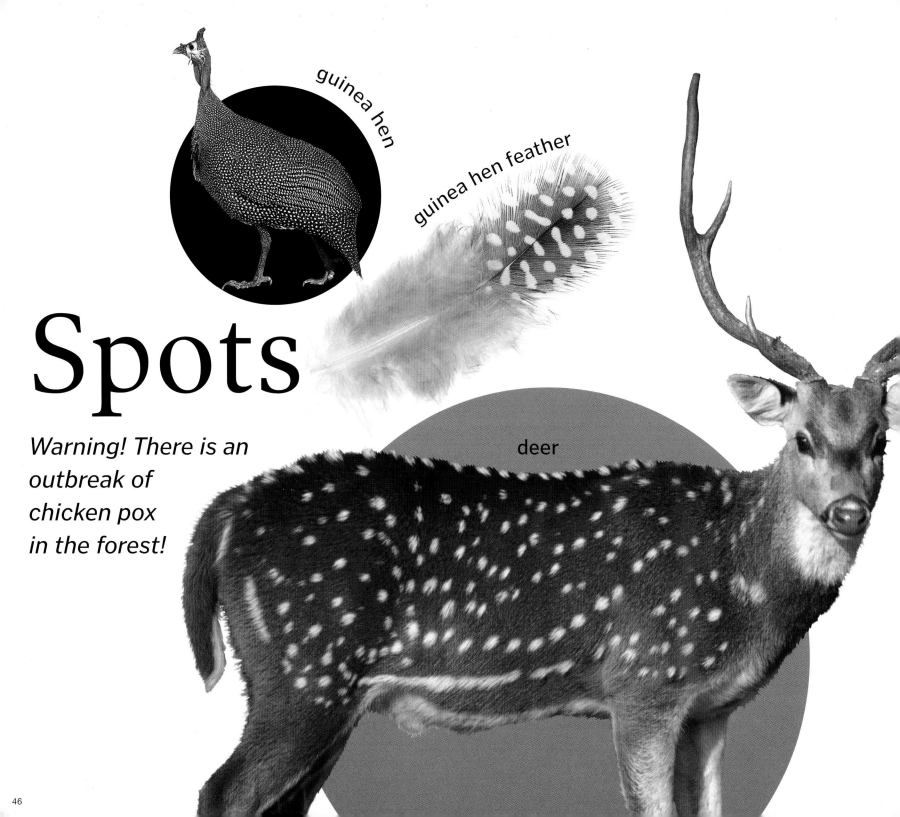

guinea hen

guinea hen feather

Spots

Warning! There is an outbreak of chicken pox in the forest!

deer

fern frond

amanita mushroom

ladybugs

Stripes

The tiger might have the prettiest stripes...

bee

guinea hen

tiger

surgeon fish

... but I can stay under water longer!

wild boar

snake

beetle

Stop thief! Give us back our colors!

butterfly

feather

Stripes

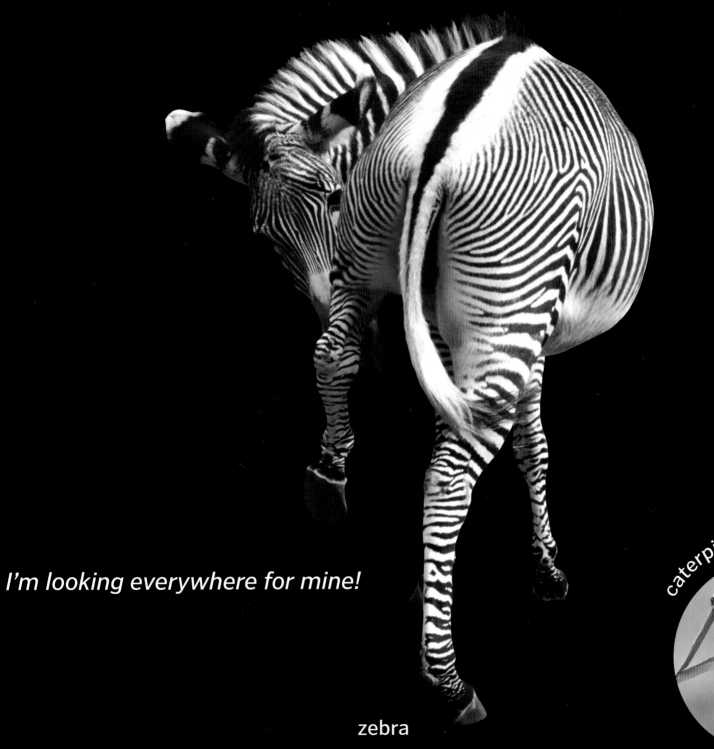

I'm looking everywhere for mine!

zebra

caterpillar

Spotted

frog

maple leaf

dalmatian

snowy owl

Who shook a paintbrush full of paint over the forest? The frog is furious, but the owl and the maple leaf think it looks great.

quail egg

Spotted

The cow is not pleased. That basset hound is wearing her coat!

firebugs

cow

basset hound

butterfly

"Is that you, Mother?"
asked the salamander.
"I've lost my glasses..."

salamander

leopard

panda

rabbit

Masked

lemurs

I don't think I have to ask, who looks better in his mask?

penguins

raccoon

Unusual

Jackson's chameleon

ginger root

sacred lotus

hippopotamus

Impossible to find a shower when you need one. I wanted to get cleaned up for the class picture...

Acknowledgments:

Play Bac Publishing wishes to thank all the teachers, mothers, and children who have helped develop the **eye like** series

SPECIAL THANKS to: Frédéric Michaud, Claire Despine, Anne Burrus, Beryl Motte, Munira Al-Khalili, Elizabeth Van Houten and Paula Manzanero

All the books in the Play Bac series have been tested by families and teachers and edited and proofread by professionals in the field.

Copyright © 2007 by Play Bac Publishing USA, Inc.

ISBN-13 : 978-1-60214-020-2

Play Bac Publishing USA, Inc.
225 Varick Street, New York, NY 10014-4381

Printed in Singapore by TWP

Distributed by
Black Dog & Leventhal Publishers, Inc.
151 West 19th Street, New York, NY 10011

First printing, September 2007

Photography credits:

Meaning of the letters: h : top ; b : bottom ; g : left ; d : right ; c : center.

BIOS : R. Al Ma'ary : 34g ; D. Delfino : 27d ; N. J. Dennis : 44 ; C. Fosserat : 43g ; M. Gunther : 23bd ; Klein / Hubert : 26hc ; J. Mayet : 36g ; K. Schafer / P. Arnold : 14g

GETTY IMAGES AEF : 15 ; Agri Press : 41 bd ; JH P. Carmichael : 42 ; S. Cohen : 40g ; E. Darack : 23g ; Davies & Starr- : 26d, 31bd ; F. Dean : 38cg ; N. Duplaix : 37bd, 48g ; Eisenhut & Mayer : 29bd ; T. Evans / Timelapse Library : 5, 24bg ; Gallo Images / G. Hinde : 9c ; A. Grablewski : 27hg ; B. Hagiwara : 21d, 24hc ; S. Hopkin : 47bd ; K.-Kal-hoefer- : 34-35- : B. Kenney : 47hd ; S. Keren : 56 ; H. King : front cover/b ; J. Kirn : 53 ; F. Labhardt : 45hg ; H. Lloyd : 19d ; P. Lilja : 47 ; J. McBride : 22g ; David Maitland : 48c ; L. Middley : front cover/h ; D. A. Murawski : 33g, 39hc ; F. Oberle : 32 ; Planet Earth / P. Gasson : 15cd ; T.-Rakke : 31-32 ; J. Rotman : 23cd, front cover/bc and spine ; S. St John : 33bc ; P. Scoones : 18g ; G. Shumway : 50cd ; B. Stefko : 17d ; P. Steyn / Photo Access : 41ch ; L. Tanguay : 31hd ; S. Taylor : 42d and back cover ; J. Van Os : 16g ; S. Winter : 9d ; L. Worcester : 46bc

MARC SCHWARTZ : 9c, front cover/bg and spine/h, 33hd, 46hc, 60cb

PHONE J.-M. Labat : 20d

SUNSET H. Comte : 59g ; Horizon Vision : 46hg ; G. Lacz : 11d, 56bd, 58g ; NHPA : 12-13

STOCK IMAGE : Superstock : 15g

OTHER PHOTOS : DR

In the same series: